P9-CBC-144

More Advance Praise for *Half-Hazard*

"When Kristen Tracy's dazzling *Half-Hazard* arrived in the mail, I had been reading the critic John Berger and thinking about his claim that to deliver the true ambiguity of experience requires the most demanding verbal precision. Berger writes about authenticity in literature, and here it is, poem after authentic poem, as thrilling a read as I've had in a long time. Here is an unmistakable talent, someone with the verbal dexterity of a Sylvia Plath, who finds ways to stay alive amid the difficulties of love and loving. 'The things / we kiss good-bye make room for all we kiss hello,' she concludes in 'Field Lesson,' just one of the many memorable moments in this first-rate debut."   —Stephen Dunn

"What animal grace in these poems of the human stumble and dance on the road to becoming human. These songs of lively observation are wise and wiser. Watch out for laughter as it rides the ocean of tears that slams at the shore of all of us ragged inhabitants, animal and human, right here, in these poems. There is no ducking the political. From 'What We Did before Our Apocalypse': 'Underneath the table . . . / we all held hands and prayed. We watched an old man insult / nearly everybody and then let him fondle the nukes.' This first collection of poetry by Kristen Tracy is a keeper."   —Joy Harjo

"There's a serious, addictive playfulness to the poems in *Half-Hazard*. The comic-inflected, subversive voice of this debut makes metaphors strike with the lightning of one-liners and turns of phrase turn transformative. Kristen Tracy writes with a sense of sustained invention that, poem by poem, gathers into a vivid, figurative fabric."   —Stuart Dybek

"If you're a rabbit or cow or mouse or human, beware this book— there is risk here for all who breathe. The cure? Embrace this book, for Kristen Tracy's curiosity and resilience, her appreciation for the collision as well as the near-miss, her affection for the hangers-on as well as the thrivers, will engage you if this sounds at all like who you are or want to be—'Love hears me coming and waits / on every stair'—and why wouldn't it?"   —Bob Hicok

WITHDRAWN

HALF-HAZARD

Also by Kristen Tracy

Books for Tweens

Camille McPhee Fell under the Bus
The Reinvention of Bessica Lefter
Bessica Lefter Bites Back
Too Cool for This School
Project Unpopular
Project Unpopular: Totally Crushed

Books for Teens

Lost It
Crimes of the Sarahs
A Field Guide for Heartbreakers
Sharks & Boys
Death of a Kleptomaniac
Hung Up

HALF-HAZARD

POEMS

KRISTEN TRACY

Winner of the Emily Dickinson First Book Award
from the Poetry Foundation

Graywolf Press

Geneva Public Library District

Copyright © 2018 by Kristen Tracy

This publication is made possible, in part, by the voters of Minnesota through a Minnesota State Arts Board Operating Support grant, thanks to a legislative appropriation from the arts and cultural heritage fund, and a grant from the Wells Fargo Foundation. Significant support has also been provided by Target, the McKnight Foundation, the Lannan Foundation, the Amazon Literary Partnership, and other generous contributions from foundations, corporations, and individuals. To these organizations and individuals we offer our heartfelt thanks.

P O
E T
R Y
FOUNDATION

Winner of the 2017 Emily Dickinson First Book Award established by the Poetry Foundation to recognize an American poet over the age of forty who has yet to publish a first book.

Published by Graywolf Press
250 Third Avenue North, Suite 600
Minneapolis, Minnesota 55401

All rights reserved.

www.graywolfpress.org

Published in the United States of America

ISBN 978-1-55597-822-8

2 4 6 8 9 7 5 3 1
First Graywolf Printing, 2018

Library of Congress Control Number: 2018934511

Cover design: Mary Austin Speaker

Cover art: McLoughlin Bros, *The Circus and Menagerie Picture Book* (1890), courtesy VintageLithoArt.com

for Alan Tracy (1977–1980) & Sheriann Tracy (1980–1995)
This all could have been so different.

Contents

III

How could she have known that statistics show convincingly that when a bear attacks, the victim who fights back is likely to fare better than the one who plays dead?

—*Attacked!* John Long, ed.

Goodness won't protect you; if you're too good you will die, but then it can be seen as a kind of reward.

—Kathryn Davis, *Hell*

HALF-HAZARD

I

Good-Bye, Trouble

I fell from a Bible. A half-blonde tease.
With a good good start, I struck out
God-filled and thrilled to claim a spot.
Here? Where? There? I touched grease,
dough, steels. Raised my low country hem.
Up. Up. I met the butcher, the baker,
the transmission maker. What next? Girl-girl
sin? Boy-girl err? No. No. Trouble came.
Pure purr. He led me off a hat-flat roof.
All swish. He spun me near a slippery crag.
And I let him, let him. It wasn't all bad.
Trouble makes trouble and soon Trouble went poof.
It's not sin or err I live down now. Wow. Wow.
But his act, so thoughtless, like a bull mounts the cow.

Presto

At the magic show I always wanted the tiger
to reappear. Did I have a pea-sized brain?

The beast was in the box. And it was impossible to tell,
but I thought the tiger looked blue, as blue

as a little girl who has lost her purse with money inside
for milk. I wanted someone to tell the tiger

it could lead a completely different life if it stopped
being so good at performing the trick.

But who listens to me? The tiger was replaced
by a lion with a caramel-brown face.

It had a new trick. It opened its mouth and received
a man's head. He put it in sideways

and it came out wet, hair sometimes sticking
to the cat's fat tongue. Bright bulbs

lit up the lion from behind. Its big fur
held the light as it balanced

all four paws on a milking stool.
It stayed steady, mouth open,

so a man would not die,
not in front of us.

What Kind of Animal

Atop his mower my father chewed the yard
while I hid with my trembling rabbit
in the garage. I wasn't perfect,
    one day she got loose. Fox,

dog, tomcat, it wasn't clear what found her.
Behind the raspberry bushes, days away
from having her first litter, my pet bled
    like a machine. Fully dismantled.

Prey versus predator. I couldn't stand the story.
What kind of animal has that kind of heart?
When our chickens finally lured a weasel,
    to keep them safe, for days I fed the beast

a small dish of food. Lunch meat. Cereal.
Popcorn. But it wasn't enough.
Not even close. Among the ravenous,
    I am a sock, a sneeze, a plastic spoon.

YMCA, 1971

It took a quarter to keep the lights on—
    that was all the machines knew. And so
my mother emptied her purse for change

while my father tried to resuscitate a man
    on the tennis courts in the dark. But the man died.
The paramedics called the heart attack massive,

a widow-maker. My parents had just wed,
    neither one knew how to play tennis well,
it was something they would pick up together.

Years later, after their son died,
    after they divorced, this is the one story
where their two sides continue to match.

They say it felt like it was another ordinary day.
    They fed the dog, then walked into
the damp indoor air, onto the invisible stick of the courts.

My father was poised to receive my mother's serve,
    when a woman cried, *my God, my God,
I don't know what to do*—the buzzer sounded that time

was up on the lights, everybody dropped their rackets,
    and began running in the dark
toward the white glow of the fading man's clothes.

Cannibals and Carnivores

The power of a mouth lies in what it will not eat and people don't
like piranhas—not because of their exaggerated teeth, but because
we fear their determination to eat even themselves. Or so the ani-
mal expert believes, standing on a riverbank, his rubber boots
pressing down the grass. And so, he says, the Indian tiger is revered
by the natives, of course: her spirited stripes, padded feet. And the
valley dwellers do not hunt her, because she will eat their flesh, but
not her sister's or her own children's. She, like us, looks at the chain
the universe has her by and nods.

To the Tender

Midsummer, and along came a hapless jay—
   blue and wobbling—flight feathers nothing more
than pins of white. It arrived at the nest's edge
   unready, which was only half the problem.

Crows perched in the oak across the street, alert,
   aware of all the world's worst secrets. Naturally
I rooted for the blue jay. Oh, but this was life.
   After the jay fell from the Scotch pine's terrible height,

it righted itself in the grass and, like a skin-kneed child
   after her first bad spill on a bike, cried out for help.
I set down my rake and shepherded the bird
   toward my spindle tree. Hopping from

low branches, it pressed toward the center, tucking itself
   into my tree's sturdy heart. For two days
the parents swooped down to feed it.
   Thankfully, the crows never came, though

I kept my eye on them. I knew their game.
   Pirates. Gangsters. Extortionists. Thieves.
But even if the world is half bad, it remains
   half good. While some of us sleep, our hearts

lie open, turned to the tender, dreaming up ways
   to thwart the crows. Yes, a hapless jay stumbles
into our lives believing it can fly, and we—knowing
   what we know—do what we can to make it so.

Local News: *Woman Dies in Chimney*

They broke up and she, either fed up or drunk or undone,
        ached to get back inside. Officials surmise

she climbed a ladder to his roof, removed
        the chimney cap and entered feet first. Long story short,

she died there. Stuck. Like a tragic Santa. Struggling
        for days, the news explains. It was the smell that led

to the discovery of her body. One neighbor
        speaks directly into the microphone, asks how a person

could disregard so much: the damper, the flue,
        the smoke shelf. He can't imagine what it was she faced.

The empty garage. The locked back door. And is that
        a light on in the den? They show us the grass

where they found her purse. And it's not impossible to picture
        her standing on the patio—abandoned—the mind

turning obscene, all hopes pinned on refastening the snap.
        Then spotting the bricks rising above the roof

and at first believing and then knowing, sun flashing its
        God-blinding light behind it, that the chimney was the way.

Urge

If a pig walks out on you—
a literal teat intact, pink-necked pig—

don't abuse yourself by asking,
What went wrong? You can't expect

a pig to care. What sparks
that insistent desire to have

a one-to-one relationship—
be it bovine or ursine or swine?

I got too close. The rumor mill
spread the story that I caught a pig

and did the unthinkable. Lesson learned.
In the twenty-first century, far away

from Broadway, people still clap
for more. They want each

questionable curtain to be raised.
Demand. Demand. Demand. If it's

meant to happen, if love is your
disease, go follow the hoof-pocked road.

Sometimes This Happens

A thin piece of ice covers the drinking trough
    and for reasons only a cow can know,

she refuses to push her tongue through and drink.
    And so my father breaks the ice with a shovel

and scoops off the slush, and the cow thankfully
    lowers her head to drink. Is she thankful?

Shit is caked to the back of her hind legs.
    A cough rolls from her throat, pushing

steam out of her mouth. Her pregnant belly
    hangs below her. A hundred other cows

stand in the trees with their brown faces
    turned away. This cow drinks alone

because something is wrong. My father caught her
    chewing on a piece of fence. He's worried

that she's swallowed a strand of wire.
    This is the third cow he's seen that will die this way.

The metal will worm its way through all four stomachs.
    He doesn't know why a cow would do this.

He pats her side, rubs his gloved hand across her
    frost-covered spine. Snow drops from the low clouds

and lands on our coats. A cow will never eat the snow.
    This one lifts her head from the drinker, tossing the hose

onto the ground, spraying an arc of water over
   our heads. A calf means money. We want her

to live long enough. She swings her unapologetic body
   away from the tub and walks toward the other cows.

Her hooves are dark and slick and as she moves she stumbles,
   the weight of her steps smearing the half-frozen ground.

Bountiful, Utah, 1972

Life began all wrapped up in the Lord.
Until I found the word *sycamore*
on the tip of my tongue.
        It was my own perfect alveolar ridge.
It was twenty-five years of ordinary discoveries—
hot pans, wet towels, the absolutely round eyeballs
of the man next door. I took in odors
        and was disturbed. I cut my finger
and let it drip. Just like that, I let go of the past
and the past's people. They walked life's short plank
and fell out of their clothes. I teetered
        on the lip of a moral cup.
I looked at the coffee bean and said,
you're not evil. Not believing in eternity should have
broken me, but I understood the saw blade's job.
        I unsnapped God like a clip-on tie.
Satan never brought his fantastic army.
For twenty-five years I cried out of hot windows,
not sure if I knew what the shape of the world
        would be at my death. A simple ball?
I sat on a hill and knew the story had its start and end.
One day, I hated my own girl heart;
it was a stone inside of me. The next day,
        this was not so and never would be again.
I had no say. I began life,
heaven or not, ten steps away
from a brick church as a half-blonde anyone.
        What I am, my soft shoreline, my need
to unlock doors and move
from one train seat to the next,
has saved me.

Vampires Today

Once, there was a year where every romance
    had fangs. It was hard to open up a novel
without a vampire bearing down on a young, virgin neck.

Soon, they were on the television. Later, the sidewalks.
    Teenagers. They owned us with their hackneyed plots.
Platinum fleurs-de-lis emblazoned on their jeans.

How do they wash them? I asked. *They don't,*
    my friend said. *It's part of what keeps them so dark and stiff.*
An entire generation has arrived dark and stiff. Unlike

my pliable, light, pubescent years. I grew up reading
    Little House on the Prairie. Sweet, blind Mary
stole my heart. Turn the page. Oklahoma. Wild mustangs.

Malaria. And Pa. Talk about a hero. Now they have boys
    so angry they transform into wild, shirtless dogs.
They are maniacs, these fans. They beg their mothers

to drive them to the theater where they burst
    into dollars and popcorn in their seats. They want the car
tossed off their withering girl bodies. Lured off

their couches, they are eager to be taken from their lives
    and placed directly in the vampire's mouth. Younger
and younger. *Cha-ching.* Is there nothing anyone can do?

Vermont Collision

If you want to see a boy lose his dream,
kill his mother with a train. It happened.

I was in Vermont serving
a baked whitefish. Her son

was busing a table. She was on her way
to buy an ice-cream cone. A whistle blew.

She got off of the tracks,
but the side of the train still clipped

her soft body, took it hundreds of feet
until she fell into a meadow.

There were so many warnings.
That night he dropped half the things

I asked him to hold. There was no moon.
It was too dark. We were too happy.

We might have been laughing
as she was being hit.

Urban Animals

I learned about Chara, an Asian elephant,
wandering the streets of Bangkok
hungry for bananas, then about

Barbara, pulling the big tent up,
wearing a headdress with her name spelled
in sequins, held in place by her big ears.

I learned this because PBS wanted me
to know about misery and Shirley,
alone in Louisiana, tucked in a zoo.

Twenty-two years of foot chains
and hose baths. *Elephants need other elephants*,
said the expert, her lab coat buttoned tight,

her purple collar crushed against her skin.
What was the point? my new love asked me
as I recounted the documentary and cried.

He felt that TV ate my sensitive heart
the way boric acid eats through the beetle's thorax.
This was an unexpected example because my love

knew nothing about bugs; rather, he loved Badiou.
Nights like this I sometimes wish I had
an entomologist to curl up with, to ask about

the dangers I myself might pose to exoskeletons.
But tonight I just want to forget the urban elephants
and arrive at something that makes me feel good.

I think I can take my conscience out for waffles
and sit in a comfortable booth
and not feel the universe pinch me

with its guilt. The women will bring them
on brown trays and move perfectly through the air,
their hips, extraordinary, the kind that children

slide out of merrily and go to school. Full grown,
I go to school, stepping down stairs
to open my classroom door and teach

from behind a plastic desk.
I talk about words and get away
from every animal floundering. Where I walk

is not the henhouse floor, chicken wire
holding me in my basket. How I travel
is not through water, hook and net

sweeping the deep sea.
Where happiness arrives, the universe and I
have a mutual understanding, I get to live

my life with this brain and thousands of one
dollar bills, which I can use however—
I can toss peanuts to the elephants or just

get into my car, my long arms steering, and drive
and, choice after choice, feel the skin
wall of my body, or not.

Unofficial Lady Bible

So many minds dwell on
    what happens between the sheets.

I wish I'd been prepared.
    Dough rising in bread pans. The fry cook

busy in the walk-in, pants down,
    hips furiously pumping against

the pastry chef, pressed against
    a mayonnaise barrel. Didn't they have

spouses? Children? Shame? The real shock.
    It wasn't just them. They only began

the parade. Adulterers. Wrongdoers. Creeps.
    How long could a girl like me work

in a place like that and keep her eyes closed?
    My role models had been delivered

from the Bible. I was handed a child's oven.
    An apron. Lipstick. At seven, I could press

a perfect piecrust with my thumb. Ta da!
    Decades passed before I would open

the door to that walk-in and arrive
    as somebody other than myself. Yes.

My busy mind opened it all the time,
    adding variety. I mean, how could Tina

commit so much betrayal? Her body
    its own Bible. Tight-assed and aging. Beholden

only to her own climb and joy. It took me years
    to admire exactly what she'd done.

Undressed

The woman in me pulls off a pink sweater
and places it in a drawer, lights
her candles, apricots spicing the air.

Part of me wants to throw this ring back,
but part of me is happy to have a diamond.
Is love sad? Part of me wants to chew the ring up

and die. Part of me always wants to die. I pick
this piece of myself up all the time, mend its mittens
and kiss it on the mouth. I love its mouth—

the little beast. A doctor on the radio
said that a woman should never split herself
into halves, *division has consequences.*

But I've quit believing the radio waves,
even though the little beast has failed to join me,
tuning in news stations for more details on every

kidnapped girl's life. Part of me is ready
to stand at the altar. Part of me cannot
imagine the closet always shared. One time

I thought I was pinned—in a car—metal snapped
through metal to get me out. After I knew
I was going to live, I dedicated my life to me.

Here come footsteps. The clamor of my lover's
shoes travels across the floor. From the sidewalk,
through the front door, down the hallway to my study.

They vibrate in my ring. A physicist might claim
this is impossible, unless my lover travels like
King Kong, his energy swinging every object

in the house. *I'm home, I'm home*, I hear him call.
(I think I love this ring!) The little beast rolling
in her new grave as he moves through rooms to find me.

Circus Youth

My life was going by. Year. Cake. Year. Cake.
And no circus. No clowns. Only that rotten dress,
    blue and tumbling. I wanted to eat the buttons.

I wanted to feed the rest—cuffs and collar—
to the dogs. Let it be dung. Let it be
    that common. I craved a ship. I desired

a texture wholly unlike my life. Clowns.
Funny rubber balls. Who handed me these knives
    to juggle? Who said everything was going to be fine?

I know. I know. Childhood shows no mercy.
Others have had to catch much trickier knives—
    all blade, no handle. No one meets our demands

for better maps or parents or more robust
Saint Bernards. The worst day of my life.
    The circus. The tragic reality that *it* was a show.

Lions reduced to cats. Leather-clad men riding motorcycles
inside metal balls. The terror of the ringmaster,
    so much like my grandfather, folding in a bow.

We took you, my parents said. And it wasn't
a lie. Elephants in chains. Painted faces blistering
    under the makeup's grease. Afterward,

I ached on my sandbag pillow. Pots clattering
to the kitchen floor. A heap of a dead horse
    melting in the field beyond my window.

Couldn't there be a different circus? Music
piped at the happiest pitch? Children so thrilled
       they shit themselves in the stands and smile on?

And clown hands, clown necks, clown thighs put together
to assemble a truly hilarious thing? Futile, I know,
       I prayed for years. Slowly flowering in my bed.

Certain of something. Wanting what I wanted.
Clown in my doorway. Clown on my floor.
       A clown on my very own thumb.

II

Good-Bye, Idaho

The dieseled fields. The lava hardened
    into unlovable craters. The buds on my raspberries

covered in frost. Idaho. Idaho. Look at yourself.
    Dotted with zealots. Spotted with cows. Luckily

this won't be like leaving a man. No scene.
    Nobody will be calling anybody a whore.

Not now. How else to say it? It's time.
    It's as if you can't see that. It's as if you can't see

a lot of things. Maybe this will be like leaving a man.
    Plopped down on a couch. And I've had to live on you.

Covered in crumbs. Look at yourself. Plaid-covered
    and mustard-stained. How could anyone take more?

Do not say that I've failed. There is a polished gun
    in every room. I dream of metal. I dream of the arrow

piercing the songbird's heart. No. I'm not saying
    that I'm the songbird. I'm saying that I can't sleep.

Not on top of you. I didn't want this to be funny.
    I'm tired of making everyone laugh. Idaho, look at me.

I'm being serious. Your trick roads, I'm done with them.
    The face they gave me. What they've claimed as theirs.

It's no longer beautiful, the sharp ways they fall.
    I am wood. When I see them, nothing inside me curls.

You think you can haunt me? You think I feel
    the same way about you? No. Everything has changed.

It had to. So, deer, shed your fur. Mate recklessly
    behind the snapping trees. Throw your brown bodies

onto the road. I said I was leaving. I said good-bye. Watch me.
    Now. My hand is on the door.

Stamps

Back when I was nearly blameless and could visit the zoo
        and admire the tigers not for what they actually were,
but as monstrous man-eaters that deserved to be caught.
        Back when I thought I had already tasted life's worst
disappointment, because I'd fallen in love right after college
        and it hadn't worked out. Back when every attractive man—
gay or straight, it didn't matter yet—getting off the bus
        caught my eye, I was a Republican. And I went to work
in Washington, DC, and met all the suited villains
        I'd been warned about. Still reading about Goldwater's
conscience. Thrilled by the idea of bombs. Strangling
        themselves in Limbaugh's neckties. Certain our own
country needed to stage a coup. (Clinton in the White House
        doing what Clinton did.) One day, I set off to buy
a thousand dollars worth of stamps. The stuffing
        of envelopes would soon follow. *The best way to get*
money is to send a letter and ask for it, they said. Halfway
        to the post office, a breathless boy chased me down.
Red-faced. Panicked. His dizzying tie slung over his shoulder.
        He told me what my boss had forgotten to say. *We can't*
use stamps with women or black people on them. The world
        toppled me that day in a business park—so young
and dumb—I left in an instant to become who I really am.

Half-Hatched

A boy didn't want to be locked in.
He wanted to blow with the prairie grass,
to feel deep and green. He was off to Alaska,
crossing a half-frozen river. The temperature was unusual,
the rain half snow. Not quite spring
and he went stuttering up the mountain in the cold,
lived in a bus. He wanted to live
like his ancestors, but he refused to spear,
stained his fingers green picking tough berries.
He waited. He thought the wet grass
would be a marvelous sight in the wild.
He waited to rush the fields,
waited for the grass tips to turn green
and whip around him when he moved.
It was never green enough and he started back.
He was writing these things down.
But he was talking to himself too,
delusional from eating the wrong berries.
And he'd noted page numbers as well, as if
it mattered in keeping things straight.
The water exploded like clockwork
out of melting snow. The streams
carried along large chunks of ice.
Standing at the river's edge,
he wanted to cross. It was too big.
His boots were soaked. When it grew dark,
he lit a candle, looked to see beyond what he could see—
and in his mind he went ahead anyway.
Crossed the river, armed with irresistible secrets
he hadn't intended to carry this far.

An Analogy

I'm saying I was wrong
and he was wrong
and that our two wrongs together
were like a river hitting
the first of the big rocks.
His tit for my tat didn't improve anything
for anyone. Except for the hikers
who looked at the rapids
from a huge distance in their dry shoes.

They saw water leaping,
something beautiful happening.
And maybe it benefited a black bear
who managed to paw an extra fish
out of the equation. Soon it was no longer
about us. The hikers kept gawking
through binoculars down into the canyon,
and the bear continued to eat.
Fish were never intended to be immortal.
Surprisingly, I had thought of none of this.
I'm saying I was wrong.

I didn't expect the wilderness of love
to be something you had to pack for.

Local Hazards

Outside Yellowstone, I see them—these bears.
    Lumbering like fathers through backyards,

ravenous for whatever we seal inside our trash.
    DO NOT FEED THE BEARS the signs say.

Even this big, they are animals, my mother warns,
    holding her hands out the distance

of a loaf of bread. *Beneath that fluff they are
    killing machines*, adds my father, raising his arms,

curving his fingers to produce mock paws.
    Season after season, they carry on. Moist snouts.

Sharp claws. Hind flanks glistening under moon and sun.
    I am too young to deal with them. Led by hunger

to my doorstep, to my dreams, they wildly arrive
    almost every day. And I close my eyes, starving

in my own ways. Bread crumbs in my pockets.
    Trout in the refrigerator. The deep smell of myself

on my fingertips. Unwitting hazards, do not come close.
    Despite your puffed cheeks, playful gallop,

the lovable way you corral your young, I must keep
    my distance. No, I cannot (*cannot!*) give you what you want.

Yesterday

looking for snails,
five students died
when their canoes overturned.

The soft-bodied snails
went untouched—never breaking
their hold on the rocks.

How much can a reservoir
hold in the dark? Ask
the moon who was not out

washing their bodies with light.
One student survived,
and he might grow up

to be a scientist with tremendous drive—
feel a need to get a move on
and figure out his atoms,

how they fly, how they stay
peaceably intact. The paper said
with all of their gear

they sank like rocks. Except
for the survivor who had been
asleep on his pack. The parents

are blaming themselves,
but they still want answers.
Yesterday, a mother broke

a stone on a stone
to see its center, and found
an ordinary middle.

When Fate Is Looking for You

A girl I knew in college was eaten
by a lion in Africa. Which could happen to you,

right as your life is happening. Its teeth
could have met the pink of your own spine, the one

your mother has slapped into good posture since
kindergarten, the spine still humming electric

with optimism and possibilities. It's your brain
that the spine heads to, a brain that may remember

the television late at night running static
on an empty channel. Everyone is in bed, the television

didn't get turned off, and you, conductor of voltage
out of the carpet fibers, touch it and are shocked.

Feel the buzz running down your spine as you
flip to the station showing animals eating their prey.

Sometimes, just one wildebeest goes down while
the entire pack thunders out of the camera's view.

Colleen wasn't looking for this kind of ending.
When it pounced, she could have been reminiscing

about her early days in Alhambra, the weight of her
blue school uniform gone for good. Or maybe she was

stringing nets into a wide stream all wrong—thinking—
I don't have the hands for this, but I will try it again.

And the lion might have just been looking
to scare things, this might not have been deliberate.

Never approach a church at a moment like this
and expect those gathered to be ready to sing.

Having It?

The story likes to end with a body.
    He cuts her open, takes the knife

to the bone, but finds her
    to be just like any other goose.

I like to think she made the golden eggs
    to bridge their lives. Why not admit

that we all do extraordinary things
    for money and love?

Today the goose is made of steel.
    She isn't that rare. And we've quit

trying to dismantle her magic body; rather,
    we're trying to predict when the next egg

will fall. Sometimes people kill for it.
    That's how want works. Sometimes the goose

is disguised, sometimes a sign is posted
    letting everyone know that the driver or cashier

is carrying a goose holding less than
    twenty dollars. Luckily, for everyone, the real goose

is dead and imaginary, or the greedy among us
    would be invading every farm, sorting through

even the clucking hens, turning their beds
    over, tossing them around by

their feet. We'd be feeling inside them
   with an oily glove, wanting the eggs

to be our miracle, certain their existence
   had nothing to do with love.

Contemplating Light

Tonight the moon is perfect. She beams on every West Coast city—whole—entirely the moon. Jane Austen is lining somebody's shelf, and it is likely that a silverfish has slipped into a binding again, to thrive on the starch. And even though the silverfish is the exact shape of a crescent moon, we should not blame the moon. She may dissolve. Astronauts have tried to break the moon, have kicked her under their hard boots, have drilled tokens out of her, have plunged a flagpole in her side. I know I am not the moon. Her light bounces off of my lit TV. She is giving me something. A way to follow the bleached stones home. My canary in her cage is under a dark cloth. It is night and she cannot take the moon. It makes her stir. It makes her cry and toss seeds and husks from her cage onto the floor. Her hard beak glistens, her tongue rolls over. She craves a darker night.

Breaking

The cats seemed to understand
that we didn't love them—
    barely loved each other—

and that we wouldn't be lasting long.
    We caught them from behind,

put them in our trunk. We weren't
cruel. They were placed
    in a cozy box. You

found a large rock to go
    on top. Everything was safe

as we rattled to the pound. *And are*
these your cats? asked the man
    at the pound. *No, they aren't*, I said,

they were just cats, we were just a couple
    who'd found them. Really,

they were my grandmother's farm cats—
thin, sick, pink-eyed. She'd grown tired
    of pouring them milk. *And if no one*

claims them, let me leave my name,
    I said. (I didn't want them but

I'd take them.) *Good of you to have brought*
them in, said the man, *but these cats*
    were doomed—respiratory infections.

We drove—days numbered—to a hotel
    out of town. Upstairs, we walked in,

the television already running. *What about
the rock?* you asked. *I have it,*
    right? And I thought about the rock—

a small moon resting in the trunk's
    blue carpet nest. All you could think about

was opening our window and dropping it
down four floors, aiming it into
    a man-made lake. You pressed. I said no.

But you got the rock anyway. Out it went.
    I turned the channel, hyenas laughing

over their fresh kill. You said it would
be fun. It landed on the pavement,
    missed the lake completely

and split in two. You shut the window
    and kissed my neck. This is what

I know about my body, it turns
to be loved at every instance, it feels
    warmth and it wants and it wants.

About Myself

I am always sad and my garbage
         is always stinking, on a curb
not so far away. Let me start again.

I wear my sadness like a coat
         and the coat never comes off.
Its wooden buttons are fastened to me.

My mother made it. My father handed her
         the idea. My pockets are empty
and it has always been too long.

I used to carry a hankie and a tiny mouse.
         But my pocket grew a hole. No, the mouse
is not responsible. I felt all of its well-mannered paws

and they felt me. It had one tooth that kept snapping
         loose. And when I approached a man
the mouse would wink its left eye. And when I prayed to God

the mouse would crawl to my pocket's velvet edge.
         I woke up one day, the sky was blue,
and it and my hankie were gone.

I thought about giving my sadness a bath.
         But why remind this heavy self
of how it is nothing like the tiny mouse

riding a feather out of town.
         If, with my two giant feet, I could have tunneled
alongside that mouse, it would have led me

to a new world where mice die
         at the drop of a hat and everyone knows this
and, therefore, exists bareheaded out of love.

Assignment: Write a Poem about an Animal

No, I told John. You may not write a poem about
your will. If not my will, he said, how about my soul?

I said no. He wrote about a male impala dominating
his female herd. Oh, I knew I could never trust him.

The antelope was not simply an antelope; its eyes,
of course, were the same gray as John's, had the same

number of violet flecks. And unlike most impalas
this one wasn't leaping through Africa; rather, it was living

on the outskirts of a park in John's hometown.
Twenty-five and still shooting bb's into songbirds and

digging through their bodies to get his bb's back,
bragging about the women he's conquered and the adventurous

ways he took them. He wrote the poems
I didn't want to read. In his last, he gathered images

from LA streets, described the La Brea tar pits
off of Wilshire Boulevard, the curve of the mastodon's neck,

his already-sunken hind legs and tail. John wasn't sure
how so many got trapped. He wondered what kind of urge

led them into this bubbling mess. In conclusion, he used
himself to understand. Twice, rushing to buy condoms

and cigarettes, he ran across a parking lot and stepped
into puddles of oil and water, ruining his tidy socks.

They were mostly young males, he wrote, *I guess
it happens*. Which, in the end, reminded me of my own soul—

bright and impulsive with an important date to keep,
she too could overlook the dark and liquid road.

Happy Endings

I like the story where the cowboy lives
        because the bullet struck the whiskey flask

instead of his thin-walled heart. Or the one
        where the boy is thrown from the wrecked car

and lands perfectly on a pillow of grass
        instead of the awful road. I'm to the point

where if someone has to get killed, please
        deliver a clear lesson along with that death.

No random, Godless acts. No mad dogs, no
        hatchets being wielded at good girls slumbering

in the folds of their warm beds. After reading *Cinderella*,
        after observing the fat and happy cartoon mouse

weekly escaping the ravenous cat, after watching
        my fellow earthlings pull together and pound

the Martians into the rock-hard desert using sarcasm
        and sticks, I've come to appreciate the happy ending,

no matter how tacky or unearned. It's today. And death tolls
        continue to climb. You think I want the truth?

Teton Road

Bear on your path. Wolf at your thigh. Cougar
    leaping from a low branch onto your back. *Your back?*

How can this happen? On a Wednesday? Daisies pop open.
    Good Samaritans merrily travel to donate blood.

But here they are, beasts gaming against us,
    growing suburban in the mountain valley. So much

like my neighbors—hungry, apathetic, bored. A child
    was bit on the wrist by a prairie rattler

in one of the Dakotas and now she's dead. All of her.
    Poof. Even though the cock crowed in the morning,

stirring the farm and assuring everything within earshot
    that the same familiar circle had been started anew.

Even the penned hogs believed this. I can barely eat.
    Gnat on my heart. Mice in the pantry. I won't snap

the strawberries from their happy vines. Bargain:
    How about I never destroy anything? Solution: I'll stay

always in this chair. Now from stage right enters
    a conversation with myself. ME: You can't do it.

ME: I can. ME: Cats starve. Clams are sealed
    so tightly rarely do they love another clam.

But you—you've got promise. ME: And my chair.
    ME: On the other elbow of this country,

a meadow shivers, and a fox has been outfoxed,
    its leg in a trap. ME: But if I leave the mountains,

I can't imagine my life. ME: I have given you
    all these chances. Take them.

III

Half-Hazard

They can put a girl on the moon right now, I suppose.
The details wouldn't be too hard to crack.
Dangers here. Perils there. It'll go how it goes.

Earth faces venoms, disease, foes and woes.
Free of that jeopardy, she won't rocket back.
If you put the right girl on the moon, I suppose.

Some might worry alone she'll face lunar lows.
Does a girl who lacks parties turn blue in pitch black?
Dangers here. Perils there. It'll go how it goes.

Like Buzz, Neil, and other above-average joes,
she'll travel in space boots and wield a screw jack,
if we put our *best* girl on the moon, I suppose.

We'll blast her above every bloom of dog rose.
Let her farewell our bright spots along with our wrack.
Dangers here. Perils there. Who will own how this goes?

Prepared for the darkness and cut off from schmoes—
whole girl, half-hazard. On a zodiac track,
we'll put that girl right on the moon, I suppose.
Endangered. Imperiled. And watch how it goes.

Gardening on Alcatraz in July

Cutthroat plants overtaking other plants. It was new to me.
    The needs of the calla lily. The habits of the rose.

There is one artichoke growing on the island. How it
    arrived in Officer's Row nobody knows. The prison

shut down and the plants grew wild, persisted for decades.
    Concerning the gardens, I know the long story

and the short one. The veteran gardeners have arms
    marked with scars from tearing out the monstrous

blackberry and rose bushes that overran everything.
    Volunteers pulled for months to uncover the survivors.

Most famously, the Bardou Job rose, thought to be extinct,
    is alive again, back in the world, shocking rosarians.

Now tourists trickle down the windy side of the island
    on the west road passing the cell house and a steep slope

of *drosanthemum* lit up in pink. Tended by robbers and
    counterfeiters, fed by bathwater, restored from photos

these flowers are back. On Sundays, I lead this garden tour
    from the dock to the summit, again and again, month

after month—Machine Gun Kelly on their minds—I show them—
    tell them—really want them to notice—foxglove, aster, fuchsia,

sweet pea, sage—all rupturing in their persistent blooms. Because
    we should all bear witness to what we didn't expect to see.

What We Did before Our Apocalypse

We stockpiled all the bottled water we could find. We argued
     over Christmas trees until all the good ones were gone.

We drove less. We starved ourselves of carbs. We buried
     Muhammad Ali in Kentucky. We ran on charisma.

We took the batteries out of the smoke detectors so all the toys
     would work. We jiggled the toilet handle to try to fix the problem.

We let people who were acting like assholes merge into
     the carpool lane. Orgied out, we debated canceling HBO.

We packed our suitcases without hairspray and barely
     any liquids at all. We reversed our vasectomies.

We fled to the mall and bought shoes. We battled the goddamn
     kitchen ants again and their relentless thirst for grease.

We watched Carrie Fisher's heart stop on a plane. We fretted
     like bigots over bathrooms in one of the Carolinas.

We cherished Alec Baldwin and reported every rogue backpack
     to the authorities. Underneath the table at Buca di Beppo

we all held hands and prayed. We watched an old man insult
     nearly everybody and then let him fondle the nukes.

State Lines

Geese fly and refuse to honor them.
White-tailed deer graze unequally
on both sides of the boundary. But I've

had to decide, time after time, and declare
a street address, a spot I am now stitched to
by my never-ending mail. I owe so much.

Envelope after envelope, a steady flow.
I understand why some delinquents blow
the box up. Dead flames send me letters

and their clumsy sentences stick to my
thumbs. How many times can you leave
the same woman? That question doesn't

shame me. Even in heartbreak, it's not
uncommon to crave abundance. Luckily,
I think I've found my next speck of hope.

New state after new state. My heart a fist
of twine. I can't surrender. The clock ticks.
Empty suitcase, where have I stuffed you?

Forget grace. The rabbit darts over
the open road. Rain clouds gather. A man sits
in his kitchen overlooking a sea cliff, eating

a piece of toast. Who wouldn't go?
What woman wouldn't drop her whole life
into a basket, plow into the dark, and run?

Rain at the Zoo

A giraffe presented its head to me, tilting it
    sideways, reaching out its long gray tongue.

I gave it my wheat cracker while small drops of rain
    pounded us both. Lightning cracked open the sky.

Zebras zipped across the field. It was springtime
    in Michigan. I watched the giraffe shuffle itself backward,

toward the herd, its bone- and rust-colored fur
    beading with water. The entire mix of animals stood

away from the trees. A lone emu shook
    its round body hard and squawked. It ran

along the fence line, jerking open its wings.
    Perhaps it was trying to shake away the burden

of water or indulging an urge to fly. I can't know.
    I have no idea what about their lives these animals

love or abhor. They are captured or born here for us,
    and we come. It's true. This is my favorite field.

Field Lesson

A tractor tills the soil using heavy blades,
        while nine mice turn in their autumnal nest.

Nine blind mice. I counted them, then covered them
        with a layer of hay. What can I help

that I am a simple child? The world
        has shown me its lessons: here, here, and here.

Lambs in the field. Chops on the plate.
        Knives dismantling the hills deer by deer

after the gun goes bang. And there is so much more
        to learn. The John Deere tumbles down the field.

Behind it, a dust cloud rises. Nine blind mice
        meet their nine blind ghosts. Tossed

from this world like salt over shoulder. The things
        we kiss good-bye make room for all we kiss hello.

Fable Revisited

Annie is saving Michigan's state reptile,
the painted turtle—not to be confused

with the white-tailed deer, or the mastodon,
Michigan's state game mammal and fossil.

Of which the former thrives, while the latter
dwindled to bone and dust. So, more

than just a turtle, just a slow-moving invertebrate,
what Annie is rescuing is a cold-blooded symbol.

It's a tense moment as cars go around
our stopped car, barely noticing Annie schlepping

the symbol across the road to open grass.
If they are wise, the motorists will see

how the grass, too, has a second meaning.
                    Annie is the mediator who,

turtle in hand, becomes a symbol herself—
for women who insist on confronting machines.

Annie is unlucky, a woman who is barely intact.
She prays for love and babies, and by this

I mean she's having unprotected sex. She jumps
a small retaining wall to give the turtle a better

chance. It snaps at her in the field's center, wags its
head and tail like a mechanical toy operated by coins.

Annie's face looks into its shell before she drops it
and races over a fence. She wants it to know she is

trying to help. Annie has been gone only two minutes.
To a turtle, it must feel like a lifetime. Picture the body

as a machine. Unlike the turtle, who will crawl slowly
through a meadow and subsist on vegetation and luck.

Taming the Dog

Your dog arrives at my open window
filled with advice. He sees how I trim the beans
     and complains. He believes the way I tenderize

my lamb is an abomination. The neck may be tough,
but in my house we use everything. We hang
     our laundry. We beat our rugs and there is joy.

Last night, he caught me pruning the magnolia tree,
appeared beneath my ladder, fur holding the light
     of a whole moon, and he mocked me

with his little dog paws. Why would a dog want
to insult a woman underneath the moon like that?
     Wednesday. Thursday. What about me

makes your dog want to arrive? He appears all the time.
Practically walking through walls. And when he sniffs
     the air in front of me, it's as if he's taking me apart.

His snout an instrument. His wet nose combs me. And yes,
he brings his own blanket of smell. Off, boy. Off.
     A dog needs rules. There's no shame in that.

When a woman says *stay*, she craves obedience.
At the sound of her voice, she wants to watch
     that animal fall like a stone into the grass.

Tell

—an alcoholic father, a sad-faced mother,
    an uncle who died while cleaning his gun.

My students have problems. They put them
    down on paper, hand them to me and say *here,*

here is a poem. Sometimes they don't get
    anything right. Chad's sister bleeds to death

in a villanelle. We find her in the bathroom
    by following a trail of rhymes. Nobody

in the workshop wants to say what's wrong.
    This poem makes us sad. We want it

to be perfect. But the world isn't perfect.
    We suffer even when we do everything right.

I should tell Chad that he has written a great poem.
    That he is going to grow up to be a great man

who will have children who he will never forget
    to kiss. His little heart ticks like a bomb.

We can hear it. He wants to have a better ending.
    But this is what he's got.

The Unavoidable Pigeon

I see it on Cabrillo, midway through the crosswalk.
    Some people spot an injured pigeon
    tumbling down the street and think

good riddance. But how can I think that?
    I know this bird. I've seen it before.
    Balboa. Anza. Clement. Its wounded

foot lifted high into its feathered body.
    No, I will never take this bird home.
    I root for it in other ways. What a survivor!

I pass it on the way to the post office,
    parading like a governor in a bright
    patch of sun. Don't worry. This bird

will never break my heart. Not right now.
    Not tomorrow. Not next week when I find it
    hammered to the road. Poor bird.

A ruptured viola. All of its red strings
    pulled out of it. Even with big dreams,
    a pigeon can only survive so long

on these streets. Had you asked me, had you
    been a reasonable being, I would
    have warned you to stick to the sky.

Hanging Up

Today he wants me to go back to Balsa Avenue
and open up our old front door. In my mind
    that house burned down and flames took the doors.

He forgets that in the middle of making love
God cracked the ceiling above us
    and warned *watch out*. It was as if a meteor

sped toward us both. But he rolled out of bed
onto all fours, hurried alone into the next room.
    I was struck by plaster and dust. For a day

my body resembled a slightly bruised
Bartlett pear. He planted little kisses on every mark.
    As an apology he carried me up and down our stairs.

Now he wants me to go back and forgive—him
and his mother and the half-naked woman
    he danced with just once. And because we are all

stupid and wrong and have traveled with dog shit
on the bottoms of our shoes, and forgotten to give
    borrowed pens back, and slept with prostitutes

in parked cars, and robbed banks with loaded pistols,
and loved the wrong people, I don't hang up.
    I talk and wander north, listening to him under

a spoon of stars. Love hears me coming and waits
on every stair. It's hoping I arrive feeling lucky,
    with my whole heart ready again.

Hepatoscopy

Opening the sacrificed sheep with a blade
revealed its liver which revealed
everything. During the Bronze Age,

the liver was a prophet. And so
it was hated and so it was loved.
I've held a young sheep in my arms

and felt the bones under its skin
and wool and sensed that the universe
was unfolding nicely. I think

I'm a believer, that if a talented
puppeteer were to stuff his hand
in any puppet and say just the right things,

that my bones could trust.
I talk like bones are solid,
but they're not. When strained

they break. We've learned how
to save people from their bones—
a greenstick fracture, a punctured lung.

Last night somebody didn't do it right
and a teenage boy was killed
by his own rib. Snapped from its cage

it looked for its other end—broke
into the lungs, pierced close
to the heart. I now know exactly

where a person's lungs are,
even when they wear a coat. I took
a class and inflated plastic lungs

inside a plastic torso, two long breaths
at a time. We can't predict whether or not
someone may need our air. But I carry

mine with me—ready. Long ago,
people consulted such erasures.
But this is Michigan, and nobody pretends

they're in the Indus Valley. We don't
go around plucking bones or digging
sharp-knifed for the good and the bad news.

Autobiography

When I was a child
the Teton Dam broke.
Everyone lost their carpet.
    The mildew wouldn't stop blossoming.

Over time, everything got better.
People bought more dogs.
I loved the yippy ones most.
    Tiny and fierce and shitting everywhere.

My closet was so small.
I had almost no clothes.
We were rich in other ways.
    My grandparents owned a speedboat.

And here I am today, timid
around water, but enduring.
Responsibly burying everyone I love
    into that dry earth.

Waiting for Crocuses

I took the train, the bus, the clack-clack trolley.
    Men traveling alongside me, beef-like with no grandeur.

Long ties. Big shoes. Elbows in my side.
    Each day another long ouch. And the lucky couples

always rubbed their luckiness against my window.
    Hand-holding their way down the slushy steps.

Breath blooming between their kissing, hat-topped heads.
    Winter. The flakes. How long does a blizzard last?

What about spring? The crocuses? The hardy tulips
    I glimpse in other yards? Stuck in the chill.

My whole world white. I didn't love a single thing.
    This is it, I thought. I was born to be this cold. Frostbite

around the corner. I worried about the tips of myself.
    And those like me. Our fingers. Our noses.

Our small, small toes. Then came the thaw.
    Clomp. Clomp. Everything turned on its ear.

His big shoes falling off, and I loved them. Their bigness
    suddenly admirable. The tie a way to pull him to me.

His hair became my favorite thing to touch.
    I didn't want my hands back. When the day

finally came, we ate it. After waiting, waiting,
    we didn't waste a single crumb of joy.

Acknowledgments

This book has been a long time coming, close to twenty years, so I am filled with thanks for the people and organizations that helped make this happen. I would like to begin by thanking the Poetry Foundation for choosing *Half-Hazard* for this incredible honor and making the publication of this book possible. I want to thank everyone there who has been so kind and supportive, including Stephen Young, Don Share, Amy Christenson, Elizabeth Burke-Dain, Mike Levine, and Henry Bienen. My notification phone call from Stephen is a thrilling splash of happiness that's lodged in my soul forever. Thank you! Many teachers and friends along the way have helped shape and inspire this collection. Special thanks to Tobias Wolff, Ayelet Waldman, Garrett Hongo, D.A. Powell, Gail Wronsky, Lance Larsen, Darrell Spencer, Richard Katrovas, Al Young, Bob Hicok, Mary Ruefle, Robert Hass, Brenda Hillman, Tom Sleigh, David Rivard, Mark Cox, Nancy Eimers, Bill Olsen, Leslie Ullman, Sharon Olds, and Forrest Gander. Extra special thanks to Joy Harjo and Billy Collins whose writing has always lit my imagination and pushed me forward, and whose presence near the end of this journey has been simply magical. Super special thanks goes to Sara Michas-Martin who edited and reordered this manuscript nearly a decade ago and told me I should keep at it. Also this book would not exist if it weren't for the help of three people who are no longer here, thank you, Leslie Norris, Jack Gilbert, and Seamus Heaney wherever you are (I've kept all your kind postcards and notes and edits). I'm especially thankful to readers, supporters, and friends who've been there almost the entire way. Kathryn Davis, Stuart Dybek, Stephen Dunn, and Claudia Rankine, I couldn't have done this without you! I'm grateful for the fellowships and time and productive writing environment offered to me by the Vermont Studio Center, Napa Valley Writers Conference, Squaw Valley Community of Writers, the Arts Council of Greater Kalamazoo, Writers@Work, and the Key West Literary Conference. Special thanks to Ulla Frederiksen and Fred Bueltmann, who never fail at making me feel lucky and loved. I'm deeply thankful to my agent and friend Sara Crowe at Pippin Properties, Inc., whose smarts and tenacity have allowed me to have a career doing what I love, writing children's books. The team at Graywolf has been phenomenally helpful and I adore every single person that makes that place run. Thank you, Katie Dublinski for my fabulous cover. And special-special thanks to Jeff Shotts and Susannah Sharpless for editing this book into its best self. Susannah, I feel endlessly grateful to you for discovering and supporting this book. Thank you! I owe much thanks to the Alcatraz gardeners who became lifelong friends, especially Shelagh Fritz, Tracy Roberts, and Kristin Scheel, for their splendid camaraderie on and off the island. And thanks to long-suffering gardener friends who led weekly tours with me and also taught me about composting and territorial seagulls. Giant thanks to Marnie, Dick, Corny, Monica, and Barbara. And I'm also deeply thankful to all the park rangers and former convicts and wardens who shared their stories and time with me, and especially John Cantwell whose deep knowledge of the island helped grow mine. I feel like I should thank the state of Idaho for being such a complicated state in which to undergo a childhood. And Vermont, Michigan, and California for leading me toward happiness. And thanks to my dad who often helped me transport my boxes. I need to thank my furry companion, Bunny the cat, who stayed in the world for eighteen years, and sparked so many ideas inside of me. Of course, without my husband, Brian Evenson, none of this would be nearly as meaningful or fun or rewarding. Babe, you make everything worth it. Same goes for our son Max. I am filled with gratitude that this book now exists. Everyone who helped make this happen, thank you, thank you, thank you!

Much gratitude goes to the following journals that have supported my work over the years by including my poems in their pages:

AGNI, Cimarron Review, The Greensboro Review, Hunger Mountain, Lo-Ball, The New York Quarterly, North American Review, Northwest Review, Poet Lore, Poetry, Poetry Northwest, Prairie Schooner, Puerto Del Sol, Quarterly West, Saranac Review, The Seattle Review, Sixth Finch, Sonora Review, The Southern Review, The Sun, Tar River Poetry, The Threepenny Review, TriQuarterly, West Branch, XConnect, and *ZYZZYVA.*

KRISTEN TRACY is a poet and acclaimed author of more than a dozen novels for young readers. Her poems have been published in *Poetry*, *Prairie Schooner*, and the *Threepenny Review*, among other magazines. She lives in Los Angeles with her husband and son.

The text of *Half-Hazard* is set in Kepler Std.
Book design by Rachel Holscher.
Composition by Bookmobile Design and Digital
Publisher Services, Minneapolis, Minnesota.
Manufactured by Versa Press on acid-free,
30 percent postconsumer wastepaper.